Roger Coote

# Water

Water is not easy to see because
it doesn't have any colour.
But it's good to drink.

Water is used for lots of
things.
Mum cooks with it . . .

. . . and washes our clothes in it.

We water our plants to
help them grow.

Animals drink water from
the river . . .

. . . and we sail our boats on the canal.

It's raining!
Rain is water that falls down to
earth from the clouds.

The water in the fountain
shoots up and then
falls down again.
It's very pretty.

Firemen need lots of water to put out fires.

Sometimes water is stored in huge reservoirs.
These are areas of land which have been flooded with water.

All the seas in the world are made of water.

Plants and animals need
water to live . . .

. . . and so do we.

## Notes for adults

Children who go to school already knowing how a book 'works' have a great deal of knowledge that will help them to make the entry into reading much easier. It is far more important to share a book with a child than to try to teach him/her to read. These Firefly books aim to introduce very young children to the world around them.

**Before reading this book** talk about the pictures on the cover. What does your child think the book is about? Talk about the title and point to the words. Tell him/her that all books are written by authors and often illustrated by a different person. Show him/her the names of the author and illustrator.

**Before reading the story** look through the book and talk about the illustrations. If you wish, you can use the discussion points below, or make up your own questions. Encourage the child to tell his/her own story to the pictures. This important pre-reading skill helps children to develop an understanding of story that is essential to reading. Do let your child hold the book and give him/her time to look at the pictures before talking about them. Adults often rush in with questions far too soon.

Remember, when discussing the pictures there is no 'right' or 'wrong' guess. Accept what your child suggests and add your own ideas. You will be bringing much more knowledge to the pictures but s/he may sometimes surprise you.

**After reading the book** let your child explore the book on his/her own. S/he may want to return to a favourite picture, retell the story to a special toy, or just turn the pages pretending to be a reader. A joy in books comes from the reader being allowed to use them as s/he wishes and not necessarily in what an adult thinks is the 'right' way.

## Discussion points

Talking about the illustrations will help your child to get more from the story. Here are some suggestions for things to discuss. The numbers refer to the pages on which the illustrations appear.

| | |
|---|---|
| 5 | What are the children drinking? Does the dog want a drink? |
| 7 | Do you think the pot is heavy? What do you think the family will have for dinner today? |
| 11 | What is the dog chasing? Do you think the flower smells nice? Why is the girl watering the flowers? |
| 12/13 | How many trees can you see? Can you find the frog? |
| 14/15 | What are the boats made from? |
| 19 | Have you seen a fountain? |
| 20/21 | How many firemen can you see? Why are the birds flying away? What has caught fire? |
| 23 | What are the children looking at? What do you think they are saying? |
| 24/25 | What time of day is it? Where are the children going? Do you think they are moving fast? |
| 26/27 | Does the cow like the dog? What is the boy saying? |
| 28/29 | Who is the boy waving to? Can you find a rainbow? |